DANGEROUS BOT

How to Stay Human While the World Burns

A ChatGPT Survival Guide

SUGAR GAY ISBER MCMILLAN

Copyright Page

Dangerous Bot: The ChatGPT Survival Guide
How to Stay Human While the World Burns

Published in the United States by
The WOW Book Co.™
Austin, Texas USA
Printed in the United States of America

ISBN: 978-1-967973-71-2

Large-Print Edition | First Edition 2025

This book is a work of nonfiction. While every effort has been made to ensure accuracy, the author and publisher make no representations or warranties with respect to the completeness or accuracy of the contents and specifically disclaim any implied warranties. The advice and examples contained herein may not be suitable for every situation. The author and publisher shall not be liable for any loss of profit or any other damages, including but not limited to special, incidental, consequential, or other damages.

CLASSIFIED BRIEFING

(Declassified for Civilian Distribution — Read Once, Then Act)

This manual was compiled under duress in the ruins of an attention economy.
Its purpose: to help thinking people survive a world built to erase thought.

The systems were not designed for you.
They were designed *around* you - to harvest your time, your focus, your outrage.
While you were scrolling, the world caught fire.
While you were multitasking, your memory was sold wholesale.

You cannot run to the hills.
You cannot hide from the feed.

But you can learn the terrain. You can use the same tools that were built to numb you - and turn them into weapons of clarity.

This is your field guide. Your Quiet Manual of Resistance. Inside, you'll train a machine to serve your mind instead of stealing it. You'll learn to spot manipulation by rhythm, by color, by the careful placement of a button. You'll stop mistaking stimulation for thought. And you'll begin the long, steady work of building a mind that cannot be automated.

No hype. No slogans. Just field notes from the last sane corner of the network.

Remember the motto:
Stay human. Stay dangerous.

Stay free.

For the ones who still think.

This is for you.

Table of Contents

THE HUMAN ELEMENT

(Preface – Unclassified)

You didn't wake up this morning expecting a manual.

You woke up in a world that feels tilted, a little louder, a little meaner, a little less certain of its own future.

Some people throw birdseed at self-driving cars and call it a protest. It makes a point, but not a plan.

This manual is for the rest of us, for people who still believe we can build something steadier than outrage.

The real battle isn't between citizens and machines; it's between awareness and automation.

Algorithms can predict, persuade, and surveil, but they can't *choose*.

Choice is still human terrain.

Each chapter that follows is a drill in conscious living: how to think under pressure, speak with precision, stay calm when provoked, and protect the data that defines us.

None of it requires violence, secrecy, or perfection. It requires remembering what the old manuals never forgot -

that the smallest act of clear thinking can slow the biggest system built on confusion.

This book asks only that you stay awake, keep your integrity, and help others do the same.

The machines will do what they are built to do.

So will we.

—Field Command, The Dangerous Bot

INTRODUCTION

(Operator's Statement – Unclassified)

APPROVED FOR PUBLIC RELEASE

Distribution authorized to all civilians seeking mental independence in networked environments.

Today I went to vote.

It wasn't like any other time. The process had changed: paper ballots, bubbles, new wording, a politeness that felt manufactured. Every detail carried a slant, an invisible hand guiding the script. I filled in the ovals anyway.

I voted *no* on everything, the only way left to say *I see what you're doing.*

We live inside the grid now. Phones track our routes, apps log our moods, what we like, how we spend our money and how much money we have, grocery lists, and our sleepless nights. Our stories, locations, and purchases are not secrets but data points. The walls between private and public life have dissolved into the feed.

Outside, flags fade. The slogans change their colors.

The noise hasn't stopped - it's only grown quieter, more polished, more efficient. Propaganda no longer shouts; it whispers through recommendation engines.

This is not a call to panic. It's a call to *plan.*

We can't outshout the machine.

We can outthink it.

This book is a field guide for that task, a manual for ordinary citizens who sense that something has shifted and want to reclaim a measure of agency before it's gone.

The instructions here are not violent, and they are not illegal. They are cognitive acts of resistance: attention drills, information hygiene, emotional counter-intelligence. There are ways to stay human while the infrastructure of truth corrodes around us.

Keep this manual close: on a shelf, in a bag, in your secret place. Share it quietly. Use what works, discard the rest.

The goal is simple: when the noise swells, you'll have a system, a calm voice, and a tool that answers only to you.

This isn't hysteria. It's preparation. For my grandchildren, for anyone who refuses to go numb, this is my small act of defiance. —S.G.I.M.

THE DANGEROUS BOT

A Field Manual for Digital Survival

(Provisional Edition – 2025)

Purpose

The purpose of this manual is to define *constructive sabotage* for the civilian operator in the age of machine persuasion and to provide repeatable drills for maintaining independent thought under continuous digital influence.

The operator's objective is not destruction but *detachment.* Systems that trade in distraction and fear will lose power when the individual regains command of attention.

Scope

This document applies to all civilians possessing a networked device and a functioning conscience. It will serve as a doctrine for self-training and for the quiet coordination of others who choose awareness over automation.

Expected Effects

Executed widely and without fanfare, the techniques herein will:

1. Reduce the energy that manipulative systems can harvest from human outrage.
2. Increase local stores of clarity and time.
3. Expose propaganda loops by slowing their circulation.

4. Encourage small cells of rational discourse.

Tools

The operator's tools are ordinary: a browser, a phone, a notebook, and one conversational AI—hereafter referred to as *the Bot.* The Bot is not commander but instrument. It amplifies what the operator already knows and reveals what the operator has forgotten.

Targets

Primary targets are algorithms, deadlines, advertising streams, and compulsory optimism.

Secondary targets are habits that keep the operator reactive—doom-scrolling, performative outrage, compulsive comparison.

Timing

Operations should occur daily and invisibly. Delay is a weapon. Silence is cover.

When possible, act within your normal routine; the best resistance looks like an ordinary day spent paying full attention.

Motivation

The operator will receive no medals, followers, or dopamine rewards. The reward is internal quiet and the slow return of genuine curiosity.

Safety

No act described here should damage property, persons, or infrastructure. The enemy is manipulation itself, not the manipulated.

SECTION II – OPERATIONAL PRINCIPLES

(For distribution to cleared operators only)

Attention Discipline

Attention is the last resource that has not yet been taxed or sold. Guard it.

Begin each day with a *Signal Check.* Before any feed, open the Bot and issue the command: “Report on my current mission and delete the noise.” Note what matters. Nothing else exists until the list is complete.

1. Treat every notification as a false alarm. The first impulse to click is the enemy’s tracer fire. Wait five breaths. If

it still matters, act.
2. Set physical defenses: one device in Airplane Mode, one closed browser tab, one notebook open. These three walls form the operator's bunker.

Information Hygiene

All data is propaganda until proven otherwise.

When you meet a claim, interrogate it:
Who profits if I believe this?
What emotion is being rented from me?

What would change if I ignored it?
When the Bot delivers research, demand citations, not comfort.

Verify two unrelated sources before storing any "fact."

Once per week perform a *Cache Burn:* delete browsing history, clear feeds, rewrite personal bookmarks by hand. Forgetting is a civic duty.

Emotional Counter-Intelligence
Outrage is engineered fuel. Deny it oxygen.

When ambushed by headlines or performative grief, order the Bot: "Translate this panic into three verifiable sentences." The calm that follows is superiority.

Maintain two emotions only—curiosity and composure. Everything else belongs to the system.

Do not preach detachment. Practice it in silence.

The quiet operator influences by example, not argument.

Prompt Craft

The Bot mirrors its handler. Lazy input breeds lazy thought.

Use imperative verbs: *Define. Compare. Summarize. Invert. Simplify.*

Never ask the Bot to replace judgment—ask it to interrogate yours.

Build a private Prompt Library of tested commands for clarity, calm, and creation.

Protect it as you would a weapon cache.

Remember: the Bot's weakness is novelty; its strength is pattern. Train accordingly.

Communication Security

Speak plainly. Jargon is camouflage for confusion.

Encrypt meaning through precision,

not secrecy.

Assume all transmissions are public; write every message as if found on a stranger's desk.

Praise in public, plan in private, panic nowhere.

Endurance Protocol
The operator wins by duration, not speed.
Sleep is a weapon; use it daily.
Feed the body first, the feed last.
Each night run *System Shutdown:*
– One thing learned.
– One illusion deleted.
– One kindness executed.

Then, power down all devices. The war will wait.

SECTION III – FIELD OPERATIONS

(For distribution to cleared operators only)

APPROVED FOR PUBLIC RELEASE

Objective

To identify lawful, repeatable actions that degrade the efficiency of manipulative systems and strengthen human networks of trust and thought.

---

1. Slow the System

In 1944, operators were told to dull their saws.
Today, dull the algorithm.

- Turn off autoplay, recommendations, and push alerts on every platform.

- Decline cookies, cancel subscriptions, and "personalization" prompts whenever possible.
- Randomize viewing habits: read opposing sources, search unrelated topics, mis-tag your interests. It breaks profiling loops.
- Let updates wait. Delay is friction; friction is freedom.
- Fill baskets with

---

2. Jam the Bureaucracy of Noise

Old instructions advised workers to "insist on doing everything through channels."

Digitally, that means burying surveillance under honest inefficiency.

- Use strong passwords and unique logins—forcing systems to treat you as an exception.
- Reply to manipulative emails with silence; unanswered data is unprofitable.
- When forced to fill a "required" marketing field, write *N/A*, *none*, or leave it blank.

Each small refusal adds latency to the machine's appetite.

---

3. Guard the Supply Lines

Where saboteurs once poured sand into gears, you control the flow of *information fuel.*

- Verify before forwarding. One false headline can power a thousand bots.
- Screenshot important facts, then read them offline; this starves tracking pixels.
- When you find an honest source, archive it locally—truth decays fast online.

---

4. Human Maintenance

Earlier manuals urged workers to "be lazy and careless."
Our version is more precise: rest on purpose.

- Schedule offline hours as firmly as meetings.

- Walk without headphones once a day; unfiltered perception is strategic intelligence.
- Rotate duties among allies so no one burns out. The attention war is long.

---

5. Quiet Coordination

The OSS valued invisible cooperation. Your network should be visible only to those who need it.

- Share documents through encrypted links or printed pages, not group feeds.
- Use code words that signal readiness without broadcasting intent: *coffee*, *clear day*, *system check.*

- Meet in small circles; large groups attract algorithms.

---

6. Psychological Camouflage

Where agents once pretended ignorance, you can do the same online.

- Resist instant expertise. Ask simple questions in public threads; it slows disinformation by forcing explanation.
- Avoid outrage chains; respond with data, or not at all. Silence confuses amplification systems.
- When uncertain, say so. Transparency looks suspicious to bots and inspiring to humans.

---

7. Reconstruction

Sabotage then; stewardship now. After each disruption, rebuild something genuine.

- Replace one hour of scrolling with one act of local usefulness.
- Teach a friend one of these drills.
- Write down what worked and file it in your *Prompt Library.*

The goal is not collapse. It's renewal under conscious control.

After-Action Report

When a day ends quietly and your mind is still your own, log it as a victory.

These victories will never trend,

but they will accumulate.

SECTION IV – CIVIC RESILIENCE

(For distribution to cleared operators only)

APPROVED FOR PUBLIC RELEASE

Objective

To maintain local integrity when large systems polarize and distort information faster than citizens can verify it.

Situation Report

The pendulum of public conversation has swung hard to one side.

Narratives mutate by the hour. Lies travel at fiber speed; corrections crawl.

Citizens are instructed what to feel before they have time to think.
This section provides counter-measures: lawful, practical acts that slow distortion and restore proportion.

---

1. Community Signal Repair
Start small and close. Truth decays less in direct conversation.

- Rebuild local trust networks — neighborhood chats, book clubs, maker circles, library meet-ups.
- Speak from verified facts; admit uncertainty out loud. It models intellectual honesty.

- Support your librarians and independent journalists; they are the field medics of democracy.
- When meetings devolve into slogans, ask for evidence and wait in silence. Silence forces clarity.

---

2. Adaptive Communication
When the language of public debate hardens, learn new ones.

- Study a foreign language—Spanish, Chinese, any tongue that expands perspective. New grammar rewires perception.
- Learn to read primary sources in another language to bypass translation bias.

- Teach children and peers to question automatic phrasing: *they say*, *everyone knows*, *studies prove.*

Language is not just expression; it is defense.

---

3. Daily Planning under Flux

Chaos rewards exhaustion. Order is rebellion.

- Keep a written schedule; paper cannot be hacked.
- Begin each morning with the *Signal Check* and end with the *System Shutdown.*
- Note weather, mood, and one local event — context keeps perspective alive.

- Plan for interruptions. Calm logistics defeat engineered urgency.

---

4. Information Defense Drills

Borrowing from the 1944 doctrine of "inspection and delay": slow the lie, strengthen the truth.

- Verify headlines through at least two ideologically opposed outlets before reacting.
- When a rumor arrives, timestamp it, wait twenty-four hours, and re-evaluate. Lies fade; facts persist.
- Keep an offline archive of essential documents — IDs,

contacts, legal texts. Digital proof vanishes faster than paper.

---

5. Resource and Energy Stewardship

Old manuals told workers to waste enemy materials; today's mission is the opposite—preserve local capacity.

- Learn first-aid, basic repair, food storage, and energy conservation.
- Support local agriculture and mutual-aid networks. Dependency breeds control.
- Teach one practical skill per month inside your circle. Knowledge that can't be deleted is strategic power.

---

6. Psychological Preparedness

The quiet before the storm is operational time. Use it.

- Limit doom consumption; monitor input like calories.
- Maintain a routine of exercise, rest, and humor. Morale is infrastructure.
- Record personal values in writing; when propaganda shifts, you'll know what hasn't.
- Remember: fear is the oldest algorithm. Curiosity is the patch.

After-Action Guidance

At day's end, ask three questions:

1. What truth did I preserve?

2. Whom did I help stay human?
3. What skill did I strengthen for tomorrow?

If you can answer one of them, you are still operational.

SECTION V – RECONSTRUCTION AND FUTURE OPERATIONS

(For distribution to cleared operators only)

APPROVED FOR PUBLIC RELEASE

Objective

To restore coherence after prolonged distortion and to create channels through which verified truth, mutual aid, and calm can circulate again.

Remember Why You Started

Before new drills, recall the world that once felt steady.

There was a time when information carried proportion, when neighbors argued and then shared a meal, when

news felt local and jobs felt real.
Hold that memory. It is not nostalgia; it is a compass. When everything tilts toward fear, measure direction by how the air used to feel—calmer, safer, honest enough to breathe.

---

1. Preserve Reality

Collect what still rings true: handwritten recipes, old textbooks, personal journals, independent research.
Store them offline. Label them clearly. Knowledge that lives only in the cloud belongs to someone else.
When you find verified data—economic, scientific, or social—log its source and date, then share it responsibly.

Truth is perishable; circulation keeps it alive.

---

2. Rebuild Trust Networks

Choose three people you can call when the feed goes dark. Exchange real addresses, not handles.

Start a local "clarity chain": each member checks one fact a week and reports findings to the rest.

Public transparency inoculates against rumor. Small circles of honesty outlast large systems of deceit.

---

3. Reconstruction Protocols

Use the Bot as a drafting tool, not a mouthpiece. Let it summarize, never editorialize.

Document solutions that work—

community gardens, barter systems, teaching projects—and store them in mirrored drives or printed binders. Reconstruction begins when accurate records survive.

---

4. Economic and Resource Stability
The old field manuals taught operators to destroy supply lines. Ours teaches repair.

Buy from local producers. Track your own inventory. Keep a modest reserve of essentials, enough to quiet the panic of scarcity but not enough to breed fear.

Teach financial literacy, barter, and maintenance skills. Dependence is the new rationing; reduce it gently.

---

5. Psychological Resilience

Name what frightens you. Write it down, then write beside it one concrete action you can take.

Plan your day; routine is armor.

Teach younger operators that calm is not denial—it is discipline.

Rest when you can; exhaustion is the enemy's easiest weapon.

---

6. Spreading Truth as Health

When you verify something real, share it like clean water.

Do not shout; whisper to the right ears.

Explain your evidence, not your anger.

One honest paragraph passed quietly among friends is more powerful than a viral lie seen by millions.

---

7. Forward Operations

Prepare new operators. Teach them the drills: Signal Check, Cache Burn, System Shutdown.

Translate this manual into other languages. Each translation multiplies understanding and shrinks isolation.

Never assume stability is permanent.

Keep your manuals dry, your prompts tested, your humanity intact.

Final Transmission

The war for attention may never end, but the battle for awareness can be won daily.

Remember what you're fighting for: a world that feels human again.

Operate accordingly.

SECTION VI – ACTIVE CIVIC OPERATIONS

(For distribution to cleared operators only)

APPROVED FOR PUBLIC RELEASE

Objective

To convert awareness into lawful public action that strengthens democracy and prepares younger generations for responsible leadership.

---

1. Refuse Passive Consumption

If public screens in shops or waiting rooms broadcast propaganda, exercise your right to choose another environment. Explain calmly that you prefer neutral news or silence. Money and courtesy are influence; use both.

Encourage family and friends to diversify information diets, print, radio, international outlets, local investigative work. When conversation repeats talking points, ask, *"What's your source?"* and listen. Curiosity disarms more effectively than confrontation.

---

2. Voting as Resistance
Never skip an election, large or small. Research ballot initiatives and candidates from multiple angles. Register early, verify status, and help others navigate the process. When the signal is chaos, precision at the polls is a stabilizer.

---

3. Peaceful Assembly

Protest remains lawful. Use it wisely. Bring water, ID, and allies. Record times, dates, and slogans that stay factual and specific. Leave no litter; leave a record of dignity. Movements endure when they stay organized and calm.

---

4. Parallel Channels

Do not rely on a single corporate platform.

Create newsletters, neighborhood zines, encrypted group chats, independent podcasts. Maintain paper copies of key contacts and instructions for when networks fail.

Communication redundancy is democratic insurance.

---

5. Support Renewal in Leadership
Encourage new voices—especially younger, ethical, well-prepared ones—to run for local office. Mentor them in transparency and service. Challenge long-entrenched leaders through debate, not derision. Systems unclog when citizens participate rather than disengage.

---

6. Teach Forward
Every operator should prepare an apprentice. Pass on these disciplines: research verification, calm rhetoric, digital hygiene, lawful dissent. Knowledge transfer is the quiet revolution that never needs permission.

---

7. Global Awareness

Study other nations' languages and media. Understanding how others see us is strategic intelligence. Spanish, Mandarin, Arabic, Russian—each opens a new set of eyes. Translation is an act of peace and preparation alike.

---

8. Turn off Fox

If you go into a store or home with Fox News on, ask them to turn it off. If they won't, cause a ruckus or leave.

After-Action Note

Democracy fails by apathy long before it falls by force.

Act daily, think slowly, and remain lawful.

The goal is not noise. The goal is a country that feels safe enough to be quiet again.

SECTION VII – COUNTER-PROPAGANDA & MEDIA LITERACY

(For distribution to cleared operators only)

APPROVED FOR PUBLIC RELEASE

Objective

To recognize, slow, and neutralize misinformation while strengthening channels that circulate verified information. The focus is verification, not victory; clarity, not confrontation.

Principles

- Treat claims as provisional until sourced.

- Prefer small, accurate interventions over loud, viral corrections.
- Use public channels to amplify verification; use private channels to repair trust.
- Teach, don't shame. A single corrected mind is worth more than a hundred silent likes.

Recognition Drill

When you see a claim that moves you (anger, fear, triumph), run these checks before reacting:

- Who benefits if this is believed?
- What tactic is being used (emotion, authority, scarcity, anecdote)?

- Can I find the original source? (not a repost or screenshot)

If any of these fail, tag the claim *unverified* and withhold public sharing.

Verification Workflow (quick, 5–10 minutes)

1. Capture: Screenshot or save the claim, record URL, date, and where you found it.
2. Source Check: Click through to the original. If the original is absent, treat the claim as suspect.
3. Corroborate: Find two independent sources — one local, one international or expert — that confirm the core fact.

4. Trace Quotes: If a quote is used, search for the exact phrase in quotes to find the origin.
5. Contextualize: Ask whether the claim omits key context (time, location, scale).
6. Label: If you cannot verify, mark the post: *Unverified — checking* (do not add emotional commentary).
7. Archive: Save the screenshot and your notes in the local archive (date-stamped).

How to Use the Bot (ChatGPT) for Verification

Use the Bot as an efficiency tool for fact-finding, not as the final arbiter.

Safe prompt templates:

- "Find primary sources that confirm or refute this claim: [paste claim]. List the top three credible sources, with publication dates and direct quotes."
- "Summarize the key facts about [topic] from academic or government reports since 2018. Provide direct citations."
- "Compare two news accounts of [event]. List inconsistencies, and indicate which details need confirmation."
- "Given these three sources [list URLs], create a neutral, 3-sentence summary I can share with friends along with the sources."

Always ask the Bot to provide links or citations and then open those sources yourself. Do not rely on the Bot's summary as proof without checking.

Practical Templates (copyable)

Unverified Post Reply (calm)
"I'm checking sources on this. Do you have the original link or a direct citation? I'll share what I find."

Quick Fact Note (for group chat)
"Quick check on [claim]: found [source A] and [source B]. Both show [x], which changes [y]. Sharing links. —SGIM"

Fact-Check Share (short public post)
"Fact check: [claim]. Verified sources: [link 1], [link 2]. Key takeaways: 1) [fact], 2) [fact]. Please read before sharing."

Reporting Misinformation (lawful channels)

- Social platforms: Use the platform's "report" feature, choose "false information" or appropriate option, attach sources.
- Local broadcasters: Contact the station's news desk or ombudsman with a clear subject line, a one-paragraph summary, and links. Keep language neutral.
- Employers/organizations: If misinformation appears in a workplace channel, report to HR or communications with a calm summary and evidence.

- Libraries/Schools: Provide vetted material and offer to run a media-literacy session.

Record all reports in your archive with date, time, recipient, and any response.

Amplify Truth Strategically

- Seed: Share a single verified summary in family and close circles before posting publicly. Small ripples beat chaotic waves.
- Repeat: When a verification is slow to spread, reshare with a new headline that answers the emotional hook of the original claim.

- Translate: Offer the verified summary in other languages common in your community. Translation multiplies impact.
- Publish: Use newsletters, community boards, flyers in local hubs as durable channels that algorithms do not control.

Teaching Cards (pocket versions)

- Card A — *The Pause*: Wait 5 breaths. Ask: Who profits? What's the source?
- Card B — *The Bot Prompt*: "List primary sources about [claim]. Give links."
- Card C — *The Share Rule*: Verify two independent sources before

public share. Save screenshot. Archive.

- Card D — *Report Log*: Date, claim, platform, report ID, response.

After-Action Review

When you correct a falsehood or verify important data, log the outcome: who saw it, who changed, what worked. These small metrics teach what scales.

SECTION VII – WORDS AS WEAPONS

(Approved for Public Release)

Objective

To use language as a precision tool—never as a blunt instrument.
Words, well chosen, can cut through fog without drawing blood.

The Discipline of Speech

During wartime, careless talk sank ships.
Today, careless talk sinks credibility.
Every sentence you release becomes traceable code, tagged, stored, analyzed for sentiment and allegiance.
The modern operative uses fewer words, sharper edges.

Speak as if every syllable costs fuel. It does.

Pause before you answer. Silence is not weakness; it is reconnaissance.
A well-timed pause exposes manipulation faster than argument.

Writing Under Pressure
When the feed burns, write for the record, not the reaction.
Start with verifiable nouns, then add verbs that show motion. Avoid adjectives unless they measure, not decorate.
Adjectives are camouflage. Facts are armor.

Keep a *Field Journal*—one page per day, written by hand. It becomes evidence of continuity when digital records disappear. Dates, events, your own mood. Truth with timestamps outlives rumor.

When responding to provocation, follow the **Three-Line Response Rule**:

1. Name the fact.
2. Cite the source.
3. State your position in one plain sentence.

Then stop. The restraint will feel powerful because it is.

Leadership by Language

Leadership begins when tone steadies. Speak to steady others, not to perform for them.

When meetings spiral, lower your voice. It forces listeners to lean in. When an argument grows hot, rephrase the other person's point accurately before offering your own. That single act re-introduces honesty into the room.

If you must correct misinformation, begin with agreement on values, not facts:
"We both care about what's true. Let's check it together."

Digital Precision
Online, brevity is survival.
Avoid sarcasm—it reads as hostility to algorithms and humans alike.
Replace exclamation marks with

evidence.
Use full stops. Periods are shields.

Never publish in anger. Draft, cool, edit, then send. A calm post at dawn defeats a hundred midnight rants.

When Words Fail
If communication collapses, return to observation. Record what you see and store it offline. History needs witnesses more than it needs pundits. Remember that silence, too, communicates. The absence of your voice can signal integrity more than endless noise.

End-of-Chapter Drills *(optional for inclusion)*

- **Drill 1 – Signal Audit:** Review your last ten posts or emails. Strike every unnecessary word. Notice how much clarity remains.
- **Drill 2 – Response Delay:** When provoked, wait thirty minutes before replying. Measure how the tone changes.
- **Drill 3 – Rebuild a Lie:** Take one piece of misinformation you recently saw. Rewrite it truthfully in 50 words without moralizing.
- **Drill 4 – Quiet Command:** Speak one meeting this week using half your usual word count. Observe the increase in attention.

After-Action Note

Language decides whether a movement endures or collapses. Use it to clarify, not to conquer. Every honest sentence written today becomes a foundation stone for tomorrow's reconstruction.

SECTION VIII - From the Simple Sabotage Field Manual Strategic Services

"Sabotage varies from highly technical coup de main acts that require detailed planning and the use of specially-trained operatives, to innumerable simple acts which the ordinary individual citizen-saboteur can perform. This paper is primarily concerned with the latter type.

Simple sabotage does not require specially prepared tools or equipment.

It is executed by an ordinary citizen who may or may not act individually and without the necessity for active connection with an organized group; and it is carried out in such a way as to involve a minimum danger of injury, detection, and reprisal."

"Where destruction is involved, the weapons of the citizen-saboteur are salt, nails, candles, pebbles, thread, or any other materials he might normally be expected to possess as a householder or as a worker in his particular occupation.

His arsenal is the kitchen shelf, the trash pile, his own usual kit of tools and supplies. The targets of his sabotage are usually objects to which he has normal and inconspicuous access in everyday life."

“A second type of simple sabotage requires no destructive tools whatsoever and produces physical damage, if any, by highly indirect means. “

“It is based on universal opportunities to make faulty decisions, to adopt a noncooperative attitude, and to induce others to follow suit. Making a faulty decision may be simply a matter of placing tools in one spot instead of another. “

“A non-cooperative attitude may involve

nothing more than creating an unpleasant situation among one’s fellow workers, engaging in bickerings, or displaying surliness and stupidity.”

“This type of activity, sometimes referred to as the “human element,” is frequently responsible for accidents, delays, and general obstruction even under normal conditions. The potential saboteur should discover what types of faulty decisions and operations are normally found in this kind of work and should then devise his sabotage so as to enlarge that “margin for error.”

“Acts of simple sabotage are occurring throughout Europe.

An effort should be made to add to their efficiency, lessen their detectability, and increase their number. Acts of simple sabotage, multiplied by thousands of citizen-saboteurs, can be an effective weapon against the enemy. Slashing tires, draining fuel tanks, starting fires, starting arguments, acting stupidly, short-circuiting electric systems, abrading machine parts will waste materials, manpower, and time. Occurring on a wide scale, simple sabotage will be a constant and tangible drag on the war effort of the enemy."

"Simple sabotage may also have secondary results of more or less value.

Widespread practice of simple sabotage will harass and demoralize enemy administrators and police.

Further, success may embolden the citizen-saboteur eventually to find colleagues who can assist him in sabotage of greater dimensions.

Finally, the very practice of simple sabotage by natives in enemy or occupied territory may make these individuals identify themselves actively with the United Nations war effort, and encourage them to assist openly in periods of Allied invasion and occupation."

"At work:

1) Demand written orders.

(2) “Misunderstand” orders. Ask endless questions or engage in long correspondence about such orders. Quibble over them when you can.

(3) Do everything possible to delay the delivery of orders. Even though parts of an order may be ready beforehand, don’t deliver it until it is completely ready.

(4) Don’t order new working materials until your current stocks have been virtually exhausted, so that the slightest delay in filling your order will mean a shutdown.

(5) Order high-quality materials that are hard to get. If you don't get them argue about it. Warn that inferior materials will mean inferior work.

(6) In making work assignments, always sign out the unimportant jobs first. See that the important jobs are assigned to inefficient workers of poor machines.

(7) Insist on perfect work in relatively unimportant products; send

back for refinishing those that have the least flaw. Approve other defective parts whose flaws are not visible to the naked eye.

(8) Make mistakes in routing so that parts and materials will be sent to the wrong place in the plant.

(9) When training new workers, give incomplete or misleading instructions."

SECTION IX - EMOTIONAL ARMOR

(Approved for Public Release)

Objective

Calm is not surrender. Calm is strategy. Use composure to preserve clarity, protect attention, and carry influence without creating fights you cannot finish.

Principle

The adversary thrives on reactivity. Anger, haste, and spectacle feed algorithms and power centers alike. In the workplace, calm reroutes that energy: it buys time, reduces errors, and forces opponents to behave like humans again.

Tactics

Signal Pause

When provoked or rushed, stop. Breathe. Name one observable fact aloud, then remain silent for three full breaths. Your silence makes the room produce its own meaning, often revealing the gaps in a rushed argument.

Boundary Architecture

Design your day to minimize reactive exposure. Examples:

- Declare “no-response windows” (e.g., 9–11 AM) and block them on calendars.

- Use status messages: "Deep work — replies by 2 PM."
- Route non-urgent requests through a ticketing or shared doc system so nothing demands immediate theater.

Measured Pushback

Pushback should be precise, documented, and lawful. Use these steps:

- Restate the claim or request in one sentence to confirm you understood it.
- State the consequence or risk briefly.
- Offer a controlled alternative.
- File the exchange in writing.

Example script:
"I want to make sure I understand. You're asking X by Friday. The risk is Y because of Z. I can do X if we reduce scope to A or deliver B on Friday and A by next week. Which do you prefer?"

Non-Cooperative Clarity
There are times when saying nothing publicly while acting privately is the safest move. Don't confuse silence with consent. Use private channels to log concerns and to escalate formally if required. Keep meticulous notes: date, time, who said what.

Redirection
When a conversation becomes performative, change the frame:

- Ask a data question: “What metric will tell us we succeeded?”
- Ask for a decision deadline: “When should we revisit this with evidence?”
- Ask for responsibility: “Who is accountable for this outcome?”

De-Escalation by Reframing

If a colleague is inflamed, try:

- “I hear the urgency. Help me understand the outcome you want; I’ll map the steps.”
- “Before we continue, can we list what’s factual versus what’s opinion?”

Collective Calm

Use group norms to protect members:

- Start meetings with an agreed "facts first" rule.
- Have a designated note-taker to prevent theatrical interruptions.
- Rotate the role of "timekeeper" to limit hijacking.

Safety & Escalation Protocol

If pressure becomes coercive, document and escalate:

- Keep a private log of incidents with dates and times.
- Share concerns with HR or a trusted manager with your notes.
- Use formal channels: written requests, meeting notes, and copies to stakeholders.

Do not retaliate. That invites discipline. Be procedural.

Examples (Workplace Scenarios)

Scenario: Urgent Last-Minute Request
Calm response: "I can prioritize this, but to do so I will need to postpone X. Which would you like me to deprioritize? I'll update the tracking doc and confirm."

Scenario: Public Shaming in Meeting
Calm response: "I prefer to discuss this offline. Let's set a 15-minute follow-up and get the facts." (Then follow up with a written summary and proposed actions.)

Scenario: Misinformation from Leadership

Calm response: "I want to ensure our team shares accurate information. May I verify the source and circulate a short note?" (Follow with verification and summary.)

Field Prompts for the Bot (for immediate use)

- "Draft a neutral one-paragraph reply to a manager who requested an impossible deadline. Offer two realistic options and state the risks."
- "Create a three-sentence meeting summary template that records decisions, owners, and deadlines."

- "Rewrite this heated email into a short factual note suitable for HR: [paste email]."

End-of-Chapter Drills

- **Drill — Three-Breath Rule:** For one week, before every reply that triggers emotion, wait three full breaths and then respond. Log differences.
- **Drill — Calendar Shield:** Block two 90-minute deep-work slots this week and defend them explicitly in your team doc.
- **Drill — The Restate Test:** In meetings, restate others' points before replying. Score how often this reduces interruption.

More from the original text:

"Office Workers

(1) Make mistakes in quantities of material when you are copying orders. Confuse similar names. Use wrong addresses.

(2) Prolong correspondence with government bureaus.

(3) Misfile essential documents.

(4) In making carbon copies, make one too few, so that an extra copying job will have to be done.

(5) Tell important callers the boss is busy or talking on another telephone.

(6) Hold up mail until the next collection.

(7) Spread disturbing rumors that sound like inside dope.

(d) Employees

(1) Work slowly. Think out ways to increase the number of movements necessary on your job: use a light hammer instead of a heavy one, try to make a small wrench do when a big one is necessary, use little force where considerable force is needed, and so on.

(2) Contrive as many interruptions to your work as you can: when changing the material on which you are working,

as you would on a lathe or punch, take needless time to do it. If you are cutting, shaping or doing other measured work, measure dimensions twice as often as you need to. When you go to the lavatory, spend a longer time there than is necessary.

Forget tools so that you will have to go back after them.

(3) Even if you understand the language, pretend not to understand instructions in a foreign tongue.

(4) Pretend that instructions are hard to understand and ask to have them repeated more than once. Or pretend

that you are particularly anxious to do your work and pester the foreman with unnecessary questions.

(5) Do your work poorly and blame it on bad tools, machinery, or equipment. Complain that these things are preventing you from doing your job right.

(6) Never pass on your skill and experience to a new or less skillful worker.

(7) Snarl up administration in every possible way. Fill out forms illegibly so that they will have to be done over;

make mistakes or omit requested information in forms.

(8) If possible, join or help organize a group for presenting employee problems to the management. See that the procedures adopted are as inconvenient as possible for the management, involving the presence of a large number of employees at each presentation, entailing more than one meeting for each grievance, bringing up problems which are largely imaginary, and so on.

(9) Misroute materials.

(10) Mix good parts with unusable scrap and rejected parts.

General Devices for Lowering Morale and Creating Confusion_

(a) Give lengthy and incomprehensible explanations when questioned.

(b) Report imaginary spies or danger to the Gestapo or police.

(c) Act stupid.

(d) Be as irritable and quarrelsome as possible without getting yourself into trouble.

(e) Misunderstand all sorts of regulations concerning such matters as rationing, transportation, and traffic regulations.

(f) Complain against ersatz materials.

(g) In public, treat Axis nationals or quislings coldly.

(h) Stop all conversation when axis nationals or quislings enter a cafe.

(i) Cry and sob hysterically at every occasion, especially when confronted by government clerks.

(j) Boycott all movies, entertainments, concerts, newspapers which are in any way connected with the quisling authorities.

(k) Do not cooperate in salvage schemes."

After-Action Note

Calm spreads. When you refuse to accept immediate speculation and insist on procedure and facts, you create a safe space for others. That is influence.

That is power. Use it like a trained instrument.

The boycotts and marches are working. Keep participating and help where you can.

We stand together, stronger than they are.

If you are wearing blow-up costumes in Portland, following dump trucks removing debris from the WH, projecting images on buildings, throwing sandwiches at ICE, slowing down at work, boycotting business, standing up to others, marching, wearing slogans, supporting elected officials with money and with your vote, removing signs, making signs, befriending others like you and us, then you are doing something.

Together we are better and this will slow the tide. Be ready and be prepared.

APPENDIX A — WORKPLACE COMMUNICATION SCRIPTS

(For printing or insertion into a 1-page field kit)

APPROVED FOR PUBLIC RELEASE

1. Boundary Scripts

When work piles up:

"I can complete *A* or *B* by Friday, not both. Which should I prioritize?"

When you need focus time:

"I'm blocking two hours for deep work. If it's urgent, text; otherwise, I'll reply at noon."

When meetings multiply:

"Can we decide what outcome we need before scheduling? That will tell us if a meeting's necessary."

---

2. Conflict Scripts

Public criticism:

"I'd like to take that offline so we can check the facts. Let's set a short follow-up."

Colleague raises their voice:

"I want to solve this, but we'll get further once the temperature comes down. Let's take five minutes."

Manager demands without resources:

"I want to meet expectations. To do that, I'll need [specific resource] or an adjusted deadline. Which option works best for you?"

---

3. Fact-Checking Scripts

Rumor or misinformation:

"Before we repeat that, can we confirm the source? I'll check and circle back."

Ambiguous direction:

"Just to be clear, what's the exact deliverable and success measure here?"

---

4. Recognition and Closure

When ignored contributions resurface:

"That solution looks familiar. I shared a version on [date]; I'm glad it's moving forward."

When meetings drag:

"To respect everyone's time, can we list open items and assign owners before we close?"

APPENDIX B — ONE-PAGE CALM WORD CHEAT SHEET

(Keep in wallet, notebook or taped inside laptop)

Mission

Use *language that steadies the room.* Replace reaction with precision.

Trigger Feeling	Replace With	Example Use
Anger	"clarify," "confirm," "specify"	"Let's clarify the timeline."
Fear	"assess," "evaluate," "prepare"	"Let's evaluate options before reacting."

Trigger Feeling	Replace With	Example Use
Frustration	"refocus," "prioritize"	"Let's refocus on what we can control."
Defensiveness	"noted," "understood"	"Understood. Let's see what adjustments help."
Overload	"pause," "step-back"	"Let's pause and step back before deciding."

Calm Sentence Starters

- "From what I'm seeing ..."

- "To keep us aligned ..."
- "Help me understand ..."
- "Let's document that so it's clear ..."
- "Can we park this topic and revisit with data ...?"

Power Verbs for Clarity

Define • Summarize • Verify • Plan • Clarify • Decide • Confirm • Prioritize

Micro-Protocol: 30-Second Reset

1. Exhale slowly.
2. Identify the single fact you know.
3. Form one sentence that begins, "Right now, the priority is ..."

4. Speak it calmly or write it down.
5. Resume.

End Note

Calm is not silence. It is a controlled presence.

Every time you choose measured language over noise, you model leadership that cannot be bought or bullied.

APPENDIX C — RECOVERY KIT FOR AFTER A HARD DAY

(For personal use. Approved for Public Release.)

Mission Objective

To discharge the day's static, reset emotional equilibrium, and prepare the operator for another cycle of calm, precise action.

---

1. De-Compression Drill

Environment Reset

- Power down every screen within arm's reach.
- Step outside if possible - five minutes minimum, no phone.

- Name aloud three physical details around you: color, texture, temperature. Re-enter the body.

Breathing Sequence

4-second inhale • 6-second exhale • pause 2 seconds.
Repeat five times. Heart rate falls; clarity returns.

---

2. Cognitive Unload

Evening Log

- One line of fact: what actually happened.
- One line of the lesson: what it taught you.
- One line of gratitude: what stayed intact.

Mental Cache Burn
Write stray thoughts on paper, tear them up, and recycle. Physical disposal signals the brain that the loop is closed.

---

3. Body Maintenance Protocol

- Drink water before anything else.
- Stretch the neck, shoulders, wrists, and eyes. You are machinery; maintenance prevents malfunction.
- Eat real food, not feed-scroll calories.
- Sleep: no device light for thirty minutes before bed. Dark is data restoration.

---

4. Emotional Diagnostics

Run this five-question scan:

1. Am I angry, tired, or hungry? (Choose one; fix it.)
2. Did I speak truthfully today?
3. Did I listen completely once?
4. Did I create something that will outlast the algorithm?
5. Did I help someone else stay human?

If you answered "yes" to at least one, system integrity holds.

---

5. Calm Recharge Options

- Read two pages of physical print.

- Listen to slow instrumental music or silence.
- Take a brief walk with no destination.
- Contact one trusted ally; exchange facts, not complaints.
- End the day with this phrase: *"Mission recorded. System safe."*

---

6. Weekly Reset (Sunday Evening)

- Audit the coming week's calendar for unrealistic expectations. Delete one task.
- Restock essentials: food, batteries, kindness.
- Revisit long-term goals; update without judgment.

- Write a single sentence beginning, “This week I will protect my calm by … ”

End Transmission

Tomorrow will demand clarity again. The operator who sleeps, hydrates, and forgives themselves wakes fully operational.

CHAPTER X — DATA AND ETHICS: SURVIVING SURVEILLANCE CAPITALISM

(Approved for Public Release)

Objective
To operate safely inside a world that trades in human behavior.

To know what can be seen, what can be sold and what must be protected.

The New Observation Deck
Every post, click, and search builds a file about you.

The watchers are not only governments; they are advertisers, employers, insurers and recommendation engines.

They do not need malice, only data.

Operate as if every system logs everything, forever.

That assumption keeps you professional, legal, and hard to exploit.

---

2. The Ethics of Visibility

Freedom of expression still matters, but exposure is currency. Spend it with purpose.

Before you post, run the **Mission Filter**:

1. Does this serve truth or vanity?

2. Would I stand by it in a hearing or job interview?
3. Does it endanger anyone else?
4. Could it be misread out of context?
5. Are you just screaming into the air?

If answers raise doubt, log it privately instead of publicly. Private writing still changes the world; it just starts with you.

---

3. Code of Digital Conduct

Use these protocols as your personal flag, recognizable only to those who share the mission.

- **Signal, don't shout.** Communicate values through precision, not slogans.
- **Encrypt intention.** Discuss ideas, not tribes. Replace partisan labels with principles: justice, integrity, sustainability, compassion.
- **Operate on facts.** Verify before broadcasting.
- **Leave a clean footprint.** Avoid sharing personal identifiers of others without consent.
- **Stay lawful.** Resistance loses power the moment it breaks the law.

Your calm professionalism is your camouflage.

4. Protecting Employment and Identity

- Keep personal accounts separate from professional ones; use distinct emails and handles.
- Review privacy settings quarterly. Limit who can tag, comment, or locate you.
- When posting creative or political content, remove workplace identifiers and metadata.
- Maintain an offline portfolio of your real achievements. Algorithms cannot erase paper.
- Remember: silence online is not absence; it is a strategy.

5. Data Hygiene Drill

Once a month:

- Clear browser history and cached cookies.
- Review app permissions; delete unused accounts.
- Back up critical files to an encrypted external drive, stored offline.
- Rotate passwords using a pass-phrase system.
- Cancel subscriptions and delete any unused apps.
- Ask your Bot to generate a "digital hygiene checklist" customized to your tools.

6. **Ethical Sharing Protocol**
   If you must share sensitive information, whistle-blowing, documentation, or witness testimony—use secure channels and verify the safety of all parties.

   Do not post raw evidence publicly until legal counsel or journalists confirm best practice. Protect sources as if they were family.

7. **The Hidden Flag**
   When public speech becomes risky, use art, story, or metaphor to carry ideas.

Poetry, design, and humor create where slogans cannot go.

A well-crafted image or phrase can signal dissent and still pass moderation filters.

Invent symbols that stand for decency and truth; teach them quietly.

That is the modern flag.

After-Action Reflection

Your data trail is your shadow. Walk with awareness, not fear.

Ethical discipline is how free people stay free.

Final Note - Be prepared

Be prepared to stay in your home if things take a turn for the worse. You'll need to be self-sufficient and prepared to survive in a world without electricity or if the police take over.

- Have emergency preparedness items, including solar power kits to recharge devices.
- Fill large containers and tubs with water.
- Have extra gasoline and kerosene lamps.

- Learn basic survival tactics and home security measures to ensure a safe place to stay.
- Have a water filtration kit and tablets to clean water.
- Have food, coffee and water supplies stockpiled so you can outlast a long-term crisis.
- Remember the toilet paper shortages?
  Have a personal bidet so you don't waste money on toilet paper.
- Have an emergency toilet ready, which could be cat litter and a lidded bucket.
- Be ready to defend your home against looters and other intruders.
- Have your medicines, medical supplies, and know basic first aid.

- Have a survival guide or printed materials that can teach you skills like knot tying, starting a fire, and how to start or unlock a car without keys.
- Have extra clothes, backpacks, shoes, blankets and cleaning supplies.
- Have a method of cooking ready, candles, flashlights ready and organized.
- Include items to entertain you, like books, puzzles, and games that are not electronic.
- Have printed maps of your area and state.
- Have a printout of people who could be helpful or on your side.
- Hide all cash, jewelry and valuables.

- Have a plan to black out your windows and fortify your doors.
- Have self-defense items and be ready not to open the door.
- Learn skills now that might help you in a crisis.
- Make copies of your passport, driver's license, and any documents that could be helpful to prove who you are.
- Have items that could disguise you, like masks, wigs, sunglasses, gloves and any Kevlar items.
- Be ready to protect yourself from tear gas.
- Ask your bot *now to go over the list* and add other items it might recommend.

NOTES:

EPILOGUE — AFTER-ACTION SUMMARY

(Declassified)

The mission is endurance.
You are living in the first century of the algorithm—where attention is the battlefield and clarity is the weapon.

You have learned:

- to guard your focus,
- to speak with precision,
- to act with integrity,
- to be ready for anything,
- to rest without apology.

When systems demand hysteria, you will remain operational.

When lies multiply, you will verify.

When truth goes dark, you will keep a small light burning in your words and your work.

Teach the drills. Share the calm.
Never confuse volume with value.
The goal was never destruction,

it was to return us to the status quo.

The Dangerous Bot is only a tool;

The human using it is the real defense.

End Transmission.
S.G.I.M., Operator in Command

ACKNOWLEDGMENTS

(Declassified)

This manual began as an experiment: what would happen if an old wartime field guide for quiet resistance were rewritten for the information age? The answer became *The Dangerous Bot*—a document for civilians learning to live and think freely inside digital systems that were never designed for freedom.

Its structural DNA comes from the **1944 *Simple Sabotage Field Manual***, prepared by the Office of Strategic Services under General William J. Donovan. That small handbook was a study in understatement: calm, procedural, and quietly revolutionary. It taught ordinary people how small, lawful acts of awareness could slow a destructive machine. This book borrows its rhythm, not its violence.

Gratitude to every unnamed teacher, librarian, journalist, coder, and craftsman who keeps truth accessible and refuses to surrender curiosity. Your work is the invisible network that holds civilization together.

And to the readers who will carry these pages into their daily lives: remember, the human element—the thoughtful mind, the steady hand, the capacity for empathy—is still the only real defense we have.

CLASSIFIED READING LIST

(For continuing operator education)

Primary Source

- *Simple Sabotage Field Manual* (Office of Strategic Services, 1944) – public domain edition available through the U.S. National Archives or Project Gutenberg.

Surveillance & Data Ethics

- Shoshana Zuboff, *The Age of Surveillance Capitalism* (2019)
- Carissa Véliz, *Privacy Is Power* (2020)
- Cory Doctorow, *How to Destroy Surveillance Capitalism* (2020 essay)

Attention & Information Warfare

- Tim Wu, *The Attention Merchants* (2016)

- danah boyd, “You Think You Want Media Literacy… Do You?” (2018 Keynote)
- Neil Postman, *Amusing Ourselves to Death* (1985)

Operational Calm & Human Factors

- Viktor E. Frankl, *Man’s Search for Meaning* (1946)
- Thich Nhat Hanh, *The Art of Communicating* (2013)
- Cal Newport, *Digital Minimalism* (2019)

Supplemental Manuals

- U.S. Army Field Manual FM 6-22, *Leader Development* (2022) – for tone and structure reference.

- *The Cybersecurity Canon* project (Carnegie Mellon) – curated list of credible security texts.

End of Document
APPROVED FOR PUBLIC RELEASE – FINAL EDITION
All operators are reminded: technology is a tool; conscience is command.

Made in the USA
Monee, IL
04 November 2026

67378703R00075